Astrology Unveiled

Explore the Secrets of the Stars

Table of Contents

1. Introduction 1

2. The Cosmos Unfolds: An Introduction to Astrology 2

    2.1. Astrology: Historical and Cultural Frames 2

    2.2. The Astronomical Divination 3

    2.3. Astrological Chart: The Cosmic Blueprint 4

    2.4. Astrology: A Philosophical Perspective 4

3. Decoding Celestial Bodies: Planets in Astrology 6

    3.1. The Sun: Source of Life and Character 6

    3.2. The Moon: Ruler of Emotions and Intuition 7

    3.3. Mercury: Messenger of the Gods 7

    3.4. Venus: The Planet of Love and Money 7

    3.5. Mars: The Red Planet of Energy and Action 8

    3.6. The Social Planets: Jupiter and Saturn 8

    3.7. The Transpersonal Planets: Uranus, Neptune, and Pluto 9

4. The Zodiac Wheel: A Deep Dive into the Twelve Signs 10

    4.1. Aries: The Ram (Mar 21 - Apr 19) 10

    4.2. Taurus: The Bull (Apr 20 - May 20) 10

    4.3. Gemini: The Twins (May 21 - Jun 20) 11

    4.4. Cancer: The Crab (Jun 21 - Jul 22) 11

    4.5. Leo: The Lion (Jul 23 - Aug 22) 11

    4.6. Virgo: The Virgin (Aug 23 - Sep 22) 11

    4.7. Libra: The Scales (Sep 23 - Oct 22) 12

    4.8. Scorpio: The Scorpion (Oct 23 - Nov 21) 12

    4.9. Sagittarius: The Archer (Nov 22 - Dec 21) 12

    4.10. Capricorn: The Goat (Dec 22 - Jan 19) 13

    4.11. Aquarius: The Water Bearer (Jan 20 - Feb 18) 13

    4.12. Pisces: The Fish (Feb 19 - Mar 20) 13

5. Star-Spun Houses: Understanding the Astrological Houses 15

5.1. The Genesis of the Houses 15

5.2. Unraveling the Meanings of the Houses 15

5.3. How the Houses Interface with Planets and Signs 17

5.4. The Power of the Astrological Houses 17

5.5. Embracing the Astrological Houses 18

6. The Sun and Moon: Your Astrological Luminary Guides 19

6.1. The Sun's Symbolic Significance 19

6.2. The Moon: A Dance of Emotion 20

6.3. Moon Phases: A Symphony of Shifting Tides 20

6.4. The Sun and Moon: A Mesmerizing Celestial Pair 21

7. Planetary Aspects: Trines, Squares, and Conjuncts Oh My! 23

7.1. The Language of Celestial Harmonies: Understanding
Aspects 23

7.2. Trines: The Aspect of Blessings 24

7.3. Squares: The Aspect of Challenges 24

7.4. Conjuncts: The Aspect of Power 25

8. Astrology in Action: Real World Applications and Insights 26

8.1. The Language of the Stars 26

8.2. Astrology and Personality 26

8.3. Celestial Guidance for Business 27

8.4. Astrology's Role in Mental Health 27

8.5. Astrology in Agriculture: The Farmer's Almanac 28

8.6. Astrology in Architecture: Vastu Shastra 28

9. Astrology Versus Astronomy: A Comparative Study 30

10. Understanding Astrology: A Whisper of Fate 31

11. The Science of Astronomy: Probing the Depths of the Cosmos . . 32

12. Astrology and Astronomy: Emergence and Divergence 33

13. A Comparison: Tools, Techniques, and Tenets 34

14. Conclusion: A Stellar Parley 35

15. The Predictive Power of Astrology: Can It Tell Your Future? . . . 36

15.1. The Mechanisms Behind Astrological Predictions 36

15.2. Astrological Houses and Predictive Power 37

15.3. Astrology and Timing 37

15.4. Astrology and Personal Transformation 38

15.5. Skepticism Surrounding Astrology's Predictive Power 38

15.6. The Prerequisite Intention in Astrology 38

16. Astrology Today: Its Impact and Influence in Modern Society ... 40

16.1. Relevance in Contemporary Era 40

16.2. Astrology and Self-Discovery 41

16.3. Astrology and Relationships 41

16.4. Astrology as a Guide 42

16.5. Astrology and Mental Health 42

16.6. Conclusion 42

Chapter 1. Introduction

Dive headfirst into a realm beyond the ordinary with our Special Report, "Astrology Unveiled: Explore the Secrets of the Stars." This fascinating exploration peels back the cosmic veil to reveal a universe that harmoniously waltzes to the beat of a celestial drum. Packed with insights from esteemed astrologers and laced with riveting tales of the cosmos, this report has something for everyone, whether you're a curious newcomer to astrology or a seasoned stargazer. With a touch of mystery, a dash of wonder, and a vibrant, accessible tone that turns complex concepts into compelling tales, this Special Report is your key to unlocking the secrets of the heavens. So why wait? Empower your journey through the universe and let the stars light your path with our boundlessly enlightening, thoroughly engaging special report.

Chapter 2. The Cosmos Unfolds: An Introduction to Astrology

The gentle whisper of the universe is omnipresent, subtly imprinted in the glow of distant nebulae, in the silent dance of celestial bodies, and, as astrology proposes, in the trajectory of human lives. Astrology, an ancient tradition tracing back millennia, offers us a unique methodology to explore and interpret this cosmic discourse.

To truly grasp astrology's depth and potential, one must navigate its historical, astronomical, and philosophical waters. This journey is akin to peering through a telescope for the first time; it unveils a riveting celestial panorama and shifts our earthly perspective, blazing a path toward greater self-understanding and universal connection.

2.1. Astrology: Historical and Cultural Frames

Astrology, though ubiquitous in contemporary pop culture, has venerable roots in antiquity. The early Babylonians hold the title for the first known astrologers. They meticulously recorded the motions of the celestial bodies, noting the link between these patterns and earthly events. The insight was profound: the cosmos seemed to mirror the happenings on Earth, and vice versa, a theory known as 'As above, so below.' This discovery would spark millennia of astrological tradition, unraveling its influence from Babylon to Greece, Rome, and India, eventually permeating every corner of the globe.

Greek philosopher and mathematician Pythagoras further enhanced the astrological understanding by attributing mystical significance to numbers and their role in explaining the universe. It was the Greek influence that truly established the 12 signs of the Zodiac we recognize today, each allied to a constellation along the ecliptic and associated with certain characteristics.

Astrology's influence flourished during the Roman era, saturating cultural, spiritual, and political arenas. Roman rulers, including Julius Caesar, recognized their 'star sign', had personal astrologers, and made decisions based on celestial predictions.

The fortunes of astrology fell somewhat during the Enlightenment, as science and rational thought took precedence. However, astrology persisted, spreading to the East and cementing itself within Chinese, Indian (Vedic), and Celtic societies, each developing unique astrological systems accentuating their cultural beliefs.

Modern astrology, as experienced today, arose during the New Age movement of the 19th and 20th centuries, as psychological perspectives were integrated into the celestial science, spelling a renaissance for astrology, which continues today.

2.2. The Astronomical Divination

Astrology is dependent on a sound understanding of astronomy. Indeed, the functions of the celestial bodies form the very core of astrological prediction. But where does astronomy end and astrology begin?

In the simplest terms, astronomy is an objective science. It diagnoses celestial phenomena using the instruments of physics. Astrology, on the other hand, is subjective and symbolic. It decodes the celestial patterns, assigning them meaning and interpretation that capitalise on the events they coincide with, or the characters they inform.

The Sun, regarded as the life-giver, symbolizes the individual's conscious ego, character, and vitality. Meanwhile, a moon's placement may refer to one's inner world of emotions, intuition, and comfort zone. Planets, too, have attributes; for instance, Mars stands for drive and aggression, while Venus encapsulates love and harmony.

The Zodiac forms astronomy's basis and astrology's language. A band encircling the sky where the celestial bodies move, the Zodiac consists of 12 astrological signs. Each sign carries unique qualities and traits, depicted in people born during the respective period.

2.3. Astrological Chart: The Cosmic Blueprint

The astrological chart, or natal chart, is the pivotal tool in astrology. It represents a snapshot of the sky at your birth moment from your birthplace. Weaving this celestial snapshot with astrological knowledge, astrologers uncover meaningful links between the cosmos and character traits, predispositions, and life experiences.

Constructing a natal chart is an intricate process involving the precise calculation of celestial positions. An Astrologer uses accurate birth date, time, place, and the astronomical data for that moment to plot celestial bodies on the chart. The resulting chart is a cosmic blueprint, a celestial DNA detailing the 'cosmic conversation' at the moment of your birth.

2.4. Astrology: A Philosophical Perspective

From the philosophical lens, astrology hinges on the premise of a connected universe. As in string theory, astrology corroborates the theory that everything is interwoven, interconnected, and that all is one. It suggests our human lives mirror the cosmos and that celestial movements echo in our mortal lives—an existential dance choreographed within the cosmic orchestra. By understanding the greater universal tides, we, too, can sail amicably on life's tumultuous seas.

Astrology then becomes a tool of empowerment. In understanding our natal chart, we perceive our strengths, weaknesses, loves, fears, and more profoundly than ever before. This awareness fuels growth, boosts confidence, and fosters acceptance, enabling us to navigate life with an enlightened perspective.

Thus, the journey into astrology is a journey into self, a cosmic voyage to the heart of existence. As we reach out to touch the stars, we might find they can still touch us, whispering of an interconnected universe where each of us has a unique and valued cosmic part to play.

Chapter 3. Decoding Celestial Bodies: Planets in Astrology

In astrology, the term "celestial bodies" refers to the physical entities that dwell in the cosmic arena. These range from stars and galaxies to planets and asteroids - everything that makes up our universe. The planets, however, take the center stage in astrological assessments, playing pivotal roles in determining the sequences of events and personality traits linked with individuals based on their celestial placement at the time of birth. These cosmic players serve as an interpretative tool that decodes the seemingly random circumstances of life, thereby providing profound insights into our existential journey.

3.1. The Sun: Source of Life and Character

The Sun, sitting at the heart of our solar system, is considered the most powerful and influential celestial body in astrology. While it's technically a star and not a planet, it bears significant importance due to its vitality and impact. The Sun signifies the core essence of an individual, representing one's ego, self-worth, and basic identity. This makes Sun sign astrology a popular go-to for quick and generalized interpretations of one's persona.

Astrologically, the Sun also represents power, vitality, and our drive to express ourselves. Its position in a natal chart, both by zodiac sign and house, helps point to areas where individuals may seek to make their mark in the world and where they derive a sense of pride and fulfillment.

3.2. The Moon: Ruler of Emotions and Intuition

Next in line is the planet that's closest to Earth - the Moon. Despite its smaller size compared to other celestial bodies, the Moon exercises a profound influence over our emotional selves, reflecting our needs, reactions, and subconscious inclinations.

In a birth chart, the 'Moon Sign' describes our emotional nature, how we instinctively react to situations, and what makes us feel emotionally secure. It can also be seen as representing our mother or mother figure and describes how we see them and our relationship with them.

3.3. Mercury: Messenger of the Gods

Hastening through the zodiac at a faster pace, Mercury, named after the Roman god of communication, signifies intellect, communication, and the mental energy driving our reasoning capabilities. It's responsible for all types of communication, including listening, speaking, learning, reading, and negotiating.

Mercury also oversees matters related to commerce, such as trading, negotiations, documents, and contracts. Its influence extends to how we formulate ideas, how we process information, and our style of communication—whether it's forthright or roundabout.

3.4. Venus: The Planet of Love and Money

Venus, the shining jewel of our night sky, symbolizes love, beauty, romance, and value. This is the planet that discloses how we love, whom we love, and what we love concerning the aesthetic and materialistic aspects of life.

It can be said that Venus is connected to our sense of self-worth and how we think we deserve to be treated, especially in relationships. It is also connected to our taste, style, and appreciation for beauty.

3.5. Mars: The Red Planet of Energy and Action

Named after the Roman god of war, Mars symbolizes drive, courage, energy, and action. It's a fiery planet, governing our passion, assertiveness, and straightforwardness in both nature and actions.

In astrology, it represents how we respond to our immediate environment, our ambition, and the methods we employ to achieve our goals. Mars' position in the birth chart defines a person's competitive spirit, their attitude towards challenges, and their leadership qualities.

3.6. The Social Planets: Jupiter and Saturn

Positioned beyond Mars within the solar system, Jupiter and Saturn mark the transition from the personal planets to the social and collective planets.

Jupiter, often considered the planet of luck and abundance, points towards growth, expansion, and optimism. It brings a broader perspective into the life of an individual, inspiring learning, truth-seeking, and spirituality. Saturn, on the other hand, is about discipline, responsibility, and structure. It helps us confront reality, set boundaries, and form a solid foundation upon which we can build our dreams.

3.7. The Transpersonal Planets: Uranus, Neptune, and Pluto

Far out in the realm of the solar system, Uranus, Neptune, and Pluto denote the birth of the unconscious collective and the transformational energies that rule.

Uranus embodies change, innovation, and rebelliousness—it pushes us towards personal freedom, intellectual liberation, and sudden transformative shifts. Neptune signifies dreams, illusions, spirituality, and connection to the divine, while Pluto is concerned with transformation, healing, and the cycle of death and rebirth.

As we delve into the realm of astrology, an exploration of the planets opens the door to recognizing the incredible interconnectedness of the universe. We see that the celestial bodies' patterns and movements are a dance choreographed by the cosmos, a dance that we, too, are a part of. As above, so below.

Chapter 4. The Zodiac Wheel: A Deep Dive into the Twelve Signs

In the grand cosmic dance, 12 celestial performers take centre stage: the signs of the Zodiac. The Zodiac, a celestial sphere divided into 12 equal segments, acts as the playground on which these performers shine. These ethereal segments - Aries, Taurus, Gemini, Cancer, Leo, Virgo, Libra, Scorpio, Sagittarius, Capricorn, Aquarius, and Pisces - make up the pieces of a heavenly puzzle that echo our terrestrial existence. Let's embark on an exploratory journey into the depths of each Zodiac sign's character and distinct impact on the cosmic ballet.

4.1. Aries: The Ram (Mar 21 - Apr 19)

The first sign of the Zodiac, Aries, is a burst of raw energy and initiative. As a Fire sign, it's passionate and often rushes ahead with force, mirroring the freshness and urgency of Spring, its related season. Assertive and competitive, Aries heralds the birth of extreme creativity, a perfect cocktail of impulsiveness and determination, often igniting trailblazing ideas.

4.2. Taurus: The Bull (Apr 20 - May 20)

As an Earth sign, Taurus exemplifies stability, durability, and sensuality. This sign enjoys material pleasures and comforts, manifesting as a love for all things beautiful - art, music, fine dining. Taureans value security and safety, often showing resistance to change. Their unyielding determination and hard-working nature make them a reliable ally or a formidable foe.

4.3. Gemini: The Twins (May 21 - Jun 20)

Air sign Gemini brings with it dynamism and versatility. Known for exceptional communication skills, Geminis embody the liveliness and excitement of exchanging ideas. Their dual nature spurs them towards multifaceted interests; they can easily pivot from intellectual pursuits to lighthearted socializing. This adaptability, however, can sometimes translate into inconsistency.

4.4. Cancer: The Crab (Jun 21 - Jul 22)

Cancer, a Water sign, channels intense emotionality, nurturing instincts, and deep empathy. This sign is highly intuitive, often linked with familial connections and a desire to safeguard loved ones. At times, their protective nature may manifest as moodiness or withdrawal, much like a crab retreating into its shell.

4.5. Leo: The Lion (Jul 23 - Aug 22)

Typifying the Fire element, Leo radiates energy, passion, and a lust for life. The Lion is a symbol of regality, power, and nobility, mirroring a Leo's innate desire to lead and shine brightly. They're natural performers, craving recognition and adoration. However, their unwavering faith in themselves can occasionally morph into arrogance.

4.6. Virgo: The Virgin (Aug 23 - Sep 22)

As an Earth sign, Virgo is practical, detail-oriented, and industrious. Virgo's analytical mind and love for order often lands them in roles of service. Perfectionists at heart, they are known for their meticulous approach to life. But, their constant pursuit of flawlessness can lead to over-criticism and cause unnecessary worry.

4.7. Libra: The Scales (Sep 23 - Oct 22)

Air sign Libra is known for its obsession with balance and justice. Libras seek harmony in all they do, whether in relationships or aesthetics. They're diplomatic, often playing mediators to resolve conflicts. A love for peace shouldn't be misconstrued as ambivalence - a Libra will readily fight for fairness when their sense of justice is threatened.

4.8. Scorpio: The Scorpion (Oct 23 - Nov 21)

Water sign Scorpio embodies intensity, passion, and secrecy. Known for their emotional depth, Scorpios are exceptionally loyal, but they expect the same in return. A natural detective, their innate curiosity often delves into the mysteries of life. However, their secretive nature can occasionally come across as aloofness or mistrust.

4.9. Sagittarius: The Archer (Nov 22 - Dec 21)

Sagittarius, a Fire sign, stands for adventure, optimism, and freedom. Sagittarians love exploring, animated by philosophical quests and a thirst for knowledge. They're frank and straightforward, which can be refreshing but may make their comments seem tactless. Their zest for life, however, makes them highly inspiring and charismatic.

4.10. Capricorn: The Goat (Dec 22 - Jan 19)

Earth sign Capricorn is profoundly ambitious, disciplined, and pragmatic. Like a mountain goat steadily climbing the hill, Capricorns strive for success, armed with patience and a meticulous strategy. While they're often serious, a dry wit lies beneath their exterior. They must avoid tendencies towards pessimism or excessive conservatism.

4.11. Aquarius: The Water Bearer (Jan 20 - Feb 18)

Air sign Aquarius symbolizes intellectualism, innovativeness, and individuality. Known for forward-thinking, many Aquarians are drawn to humanitarian pursuits. They value intellectual and emotional independence, sometimes coming off as detached. Their active minds often yield unique, progressive ideas, but can also leave them feeling isolated due to their eccentric views.

4.12. Pisces: The Fish (Feb 19 - Mar 20)

Closing the constellation circle, Water sign Pisces represents deep feelings, creativity, and intuition. Pisceans are profoundly spiritual and empathetic, often demonstrating psychic tendencies. Their inclination to dream can lead to incredible creativity, but they need to balance this with grounding practicalities. Compassionate and comforting, they can also struggle with setting boundaries.

So, this is the brush stroke picture of the Zodiac wheel - each sign bestowing the celestial stage with its distinct flair and unique rhythm. As we understand their natures and dynamics better, we can appreciate the grand cosmic orchestra that plays a symphony of influences over our lives.

Chapter 5. Star-Spun Houses: Understanding the Astrological Houses

To grasp the full expanse of astrology, it's crucial to understand the significance of the astrological houses. These 12 symbolic domains provide a contextual stage where the celestial players - the planets and signs - perform their cosmic dance.

Let's delve into the intricacies of these celestial dwellings and uncover their symbolic significance, hosting planets and accommodating signs. Finally, you'll discover how these houses, like threads in the cosmic tapestry, shape the grand design we call life.

5.1. The Genesis of the Houses

Astrological houses originate from the very rotation of the Earth on its own axis. Each house represents 2 hours of the Earth's 24-hour rotation, just as each zodiac sign represents 1 month of the sun's 12 month journey through the signs. As the 'earthly counterparts' to the zodiac, the houses express the fields of experience wherein the energies of the signs come into play.

5.2. Unraveling the Meanings of the Houses

Each of the 12 houses in astrology governs a different aspect of life, from personal identity to spiritual enlightenment. The symbolism of each house remains consistent, regardless of the signs or planets appearing within it.

1. The First House corresponds to the sign of Aries and is ruled by

Mars. It governs the self, appearance, and personal identity. This is the house of "I am."

2. The Second House, like Taurus, is about material possessions and the value we assign to things. It's ruled by Venus, and echoes the sentiment of "I have."

3. Gemini's realm is the Third House. It's governed by Mercury and reflects communication, neighborhood, siblings, and education. This is the space of "I think."

4. The Fourth House is correlated to Cancer, and it's ruled by the Moon. Often referred to as the nadir, it signifies home, roots, and family. It rings with "I feel."

5. Echoing Leo, the Fifth House is about creativity, romance, and pleasure. It is ruled by the Sun, and it exclaims "I will."

6. Virgo's house is the Sixth, ruled by Mercury. It oversees health, daily routines, diet, and service to others. It states "I analyze."

7. The realm of Libra is the Seventh House. It's ruled by Venus and explores relationships, contracts, and how we relate to others. It announces "I balance."

8. The intense Eighth House belongs to Scorpio and Pluto. This realm governs transformations, death, rebirth, and shared finances. "I desire" is its decree.

9. Sagittarius leads the Ninth House, ruled by Jupiter. It oversees foreign travel, higher education, philosophy, and understanding. "I see" is its proclamation.

10. Capricorn's house is the Tenth or Midheaven. Ruled by Saturn, this house marks career, reputation, and aspirations. It pronounces "I use."

11. The Eleventh House, steered by Aquarius and Uranus, emphasizes friendships, alliances, and collective ideals. It vocalizes "I know."

12. Last is the Twelfth House, led by Pisces and Neptune. The realm

of the subconscious mind, dreams, karma, and the unseen, its whisper is "I believe."

5.3. How the Houses Interface with Planets and Signs

The houses serve as the stage on which the planets and signs very much act out their individual roles. The nature of the house provides context and shading to the planetary energies and characteristics of the sign. A planet in the Seventh House, for example, will express itself through the lens of relationships and partnership.

Moreover, the house where a sign's ruler resides tells more about how the energy of that sign manifests for an individual. If someone's Venus lies in the Third House, their love (Venus) may manifest through communication, siblings, or perhaps neighborhood activities (Third House).

5.4. The Power of the Astrological Houses

Understanding the astrological houses provides a more detailed and nuanced interpretation of a natal chart. It can serve as an exquisite tool for self-awareness and growth, helping to identify strengths, uncover potential challenges, and reveal previously unexplored layers of one's personality and life experiences.

Compared to the constellations of zodiac signs, the houses are more personal and immediate. They highlight the complex environments where you partake in life's act, shaping character and destiny in line with the celestial symphony.

5.5. Embracing the Astrological Houses

As you grow your understanding of the astrological houses, bear in mind that they work hand in hand with the planets and signs to weave a rich, complex picture of your unique astrological landscape.

Moreover, the houses' meaning may broaden or deepen depending on different astrological systems and cultural perspectives. Make room for fluidity and intuition within your understanding, and let the cosmos guide you to your unique interstellar understanding.

In your journey through the astrological houses, be prepared to take detours, explore uncharted territories, and make the occasional pit-stop. Remember, it's not solely about reaching a destination but instead about the richness of the journey itself. Step forward, fellow stargazer, and explore the cosmic abodes awaiting you. Let your interstellar exploration begin anew with each house, each planet, each sign—after all, the cosmos is an intriguing place!

Chapter 6. The Sun and Moon: Your Astrological Luminary Guides

In the grand cosmic ballet, the Sun and Moon are more than just celestial bodies illuminating our skies. They are distinguished avatars on the astrological stage, mapping out our personal traits, desires, and life paths.

The Sun, the celestial titan at the center of our Solar System, is a symbol of our core being, our essence – it shines a light on our individuality and sense of self. It's the kind of person we aspire to be, our personal truth. It indicates our fundamental motivations, dreams, and the fuel that drives our life's course.

6.1. The Sun's Symbolic Significance

The Sun represents the day and is associated with consciousness, asserting its radiant influence over our conscious minds and identities. Astrologically, the Sun's placement in an individual's natal chart signifies the zodiac sign that the person most identifies with. It represents fundamental characteristics, primary drives, and the egotistic self.

The Sun occupies a particular 'house' in your chart at the time of your birth, reflecting a specific area of life. It is here where the Sun's energy is channeled, revealing our call to fame and individuality, and the manner in which we strive to make our mark in the world.

Influence from the Sun tends more toward the masculine, extroverted, active, and yang side of the spectrum. It embodies vigor, vitality, leadership, and authority. Its golden light ushers in ambition, self-affirmation, creativity, and the courage to express oneself.

6.2. The Moon: A Dance of Emotion

While the Sun governs our conscious minds, the Moon reigns over the night, when the subconscious mind unfolds. The Moon symbolizes the intimate, emotional side of your nature. Our emotional responses, instincts, intuitions, and unconscious patterns are all under the Moon's purview.

Just as the Moon mirrors Sun's light in the physical realm, it astrologically reflects our inherent needs and unconscious desires in the domain of emotion. These primal needs form the undercurrent of our reactions, prompting the way we instinctually respond to situations.

The Moon's placement represents your emotional responses, instincts and habits, essentially influencing how we feel and how these feelings shape our reactions. It speaks volumes about our inherent needs and what gives us comfort. It signifies the feminine, introverted, receptive, and yin attributes.

6.3. Moon Phases: A Symphony of Shifting Tides

In the astrological theater, Moon phases play a critical role. Each phase of the Moon symbolizes a different stage in the process of personal growth and self-discovery.

The New Moon is the birth phase, the initiation of a new cycle. Symbolically, it's a potent time for fresh beginnings and setting intentions. Following the New Moon, the Waxing Crescent represents the time of growth and intention-building.

The First Quarter or Half Moon signifies a critical turning point, an inner calling to take action. The Waxing Gibbous phase denotes refinement and adjustment, a time to gather momentum before the climax. With the Full Moon comes fruition, indicating completion, realization, and even closure.

The Waning phases that succeed mirror a withdrawal, a time for introspection and letting go. They are the Waning Gibbous (the period of reappraisal), Last Quarter (the point of crisis or change), and the Waning Crescent (the phase of surrender before a new cycle begins).

6.4. The Sun and Moon: A Mesmerizing Celestial Pair

The Sun and Moon duo in our natal chart—the Sun sign and the Moon sign—collectively sketch an intimate portrait of our personality. The Sun sign illuminates our rational side, our overt self, while the moon sign gives insight into our hidden self, the emotional core.

Astrologically, the Sun and Moon are not planets but 'luminaries', enlightening our path through life. The Sun's energy is warming, invigorating, vitalizing, while the Moon's energy is calming, receptive, and reflective.

Between the Sun's outward, assertive energy and the Moon's internal, nurturing rhythm, we each weave a unique dance of individuality and emotion. This powerful interplay between the Sun and Moon forms the basis for understanding the fundamentals of astrology, highlighting the diversity and dynamism of the individual self.

The exploration of the Sun and Moon culminates in the acknowledgement of the paradox of human identity - how we strive for authenticity and self-expression even as we seek security, acceptance, and the comfort of emotional connectedness. Remember, your Sun sign tells you what you are learning, while your Moon sign tells you what you are feeling.

Astrology, in its mystical essence, encourages us to embrace all facets of our being, urging us to seek insight amidst the cosmic ebb and flow. As we tune into the dialog between the Sun and Moon within us, we tap into deep wells of self-awareness and empathy, empowering ourselves to navigate our own destinies. The heavenly dance of the Sun and Moon, the symbols of life itself in our birth charts, instills in us the courage to illuminate the darkness and gracefully sail the tides of life.

Chapter 7. Planetary Aspects: Trines, Squares, and Conjuncts Oh My!

Residing beyond the daily considerations of terrestrial life, celestial bodies spin in a tight choreographed ballet, harmoniously waltzing to the invisible chords of the cosmic song. These celestial bodies and their intricate relational dance form the immutable foundation of astrology – the study that purports mankind's terrestrial events, experiences, behaviors, and predictions are meaningfully influenced by these celestial entities. Astrologers measure these relationships in degrees, translating into aspects between planets. In our journey today, we will delve into the enigmatic world of Trines, Squares, and Conjuncts

7.1. The Language of Celestial Harmonies: Understanding Aspects

At the most rudimentary level, astrological aspects are the angles between any two planets' position, measured in degrees along the ecliptic. These angles, viewed against the backdrop of the 360-degree wheel of the celestial sphere, result in distinctive patterns and relationships that astrologers believe influence our lives on earth. The primary aspects or the 'Ptolemaic aspects,' comprise the quintessential, 'Conjunction (0°)', 'Sextile (60°)','Square (90°)', 'Trine (120°)', and 'Opposition (180°).' They are the fundamental forms through which the planets communicate, engendering vital spheres of our life.

```
TABLE A: Basic Aspects
|===
```

```
| Aspect | Degrees | Character
| Conjunction | 0° | Integrative
| Sextile | 60° | Harmonious
| Square | 90° | Challenging
| Trine | 120° | Easy
| Opposition | 180° | Polarizing
|===
```

7.2. Trines: The Aspect of Blessings

Trines, formed when planets are approximately 120 degrees apart, represent harmony and ease. They're the "good luck" charmers of astrological aspects, marking dynamics where everything seems to fall into place without much effort. The synergized elements signifying a Trine induce a natural flow of creativity and success by invoking the qualities of supporting zodiac signs.

The triangle that a Trine forms on the astrological chart symbolizes stability and balance, but this natural ease can also lead to complacency or taking things for granted. Trines encourage us to express our talents but challenge us not to grow lazy or complacent.

7.3. Squares: The Aspect of Challenges

In stark contrast to the harmony and ease of Trines, Squares, approximately 90 degrees apart, symbolize tension, obstacles, and growth. This "stressful" aspect marks an area of our life that demands action and resolution.

The challenge of a Square pushes us towards change and growth, even though it may feel uncomfortable. Squares represent inner tension that seeks outward expression, often perceived as a crisis pushing for transformation. Struggling to balance the energies of two

Squares can feel like anchoring between two magnetic poles. However, once harnessed, Squares can produce the drive and ambition necessary to achieve concrete results.

7.4. Conjuncts: The Aspect of Power

Conjunctions occur when planets align at the same degree within the same zodiac sign. They symbolize power, fusion, and emphasis. The combined energies of both planets heighten each other's expression. They're the atomic fusion of celestial mechanics where the properties blend, and a new energy form emerges.

Like blending colors on a palette, a conjunction creates new hues the individual colors could not achieve alone. However, the influence can be harmonious or challenging, depending on the involved planets.

The heavenly symphony of planets is a marvel of celestial arithmetic, mirroring innumerable facets of human lives. From the harmony saturated Trines to the challenging Squares and power-infused Conjuncts, every aspect has a tale to narrate about the potential course of our terrestrial life. Astrology serves as a cosmic guide, shedding light on the path etched by the stars. Deciphering planetary aspects unfurls the parchment narrating our destiny, encouraging us to harmonize our path with the cosmic melody.

Indeed, gazing upwards toward the celestial spheres can direct us to look inward, promising to uncover the buried treasures that reside within the cosmic soil of our souls. Whether one views astrology as a spiritual science, a handy tool, or a fascinating hobby - planetary aspects and their profound impact on human life remains an enrichingly complex domain to explore.

Chapter 8. Astrology in Action: Real World Applications and Insights

Astrology isn't just about horoscopes and zodiac signs. Instead, it is a vital way to dissect and understand the intricate patterns of the world that surrounds us. So deeply has astrology trickled into our lives that it's almost impossible to trace its outreach.

8.1. The Language of the Stars

Astrology is, after all, the language of the stars. Enveloping every aspect of human life are the vibrant threads of celestial messages waiting to be interpreted. The cosmos outlines everyday practicality, not limiting itself merely to broad philosophical questions about human existence. In every true sense, astrology is a tool that we subtly and often unknowingly use to navigate the world.

Understanding this language is akin to understanding the core rhythm of life. It is from this rhythm that the patterns of our lives emerge. Once we understand this beautifully woven cosmic language, we can utilize these patterns to our advantage.

8.2. Astrology and Personality

On a personal level, astrology provides profound insights into human personality and behavior. In the business world, recruiters have begun to see the benefit of such knowledge, using astrology to understand potential hires. By looking at a candidate's birth chart, a skilled astrologer can gain insights into their innate traits, strengths, and possible challenges.

While this isn't mainstream practice, several anecdotal case studies suggest the potential benefits to both employers and employees. To embrace diversity within the workforce, astrology can certainly provide unique and varied perspectives.

8.3. Celestial Guidance for Business

In the world of entrepreneurship and commerce, astrology is gaining traction. More businesses, big and small, are tapping into celestial wisdom for advice, be it for launching new products or choosing the best dates for significant corporate events. Businesses are using astrological transits to remain dynamic, flexible, and ready to adapt to energy shifts.

Imagine you're an entrepreneur planning to launch a new product. By consulting an astrologer, you'll be able to pinpoint a date and time when the alignment of the stars creates an energetically favorable window for a new beginning. Conversely, as a stock market enthusiast, you could track the movements of Mercury, for example, to anticipate periods of potentially heightened volatility in the marketplace.

8.4. Astrology's Role in Mental Health

Astrology has also found relevant applications in the realm of mental health. By examining the placement of the Moon and various other celestial bodies at the time of an individual's birth, astrologers can offer insights into emotional predispositions, sensitivity levels, and coping mechanisms. This, coupled with regular psychotherapy, can assist in creating more-personalized treatment plans for patients.

It's important to mention that astrology isn't used as a diagnostic tool for mental health conditions, but rather as an augmentation to traditional therapy, adding another layer of understanding and insight.

8.5. Astrology in Agriculture: The Farmer's Almanac

Think farming is strictly tied to the soil? Think again. Astrology has played a big role in agriculture for centuries. Farmers once planted by the phases of the moon, and many still follow astrological calendars. The popularity of publications like "The Farmer's Almanac" attests to the endurance of these practices.

The Farmer's Almanac contains long-range weather forecasts and dates for planting and harvesting crops according to astrological signs. Sanskrit texts from ancient India also detail similar astrological agricultural practices. Advancements in technology and farming practices have altered this reliance, but the influence remains.

8.6. Astrology in Architecture: Vastu Shastra

Architecture and city planning, too, have been influenced by astrology. In India, an ancient architectural concept called Vastu Shastra prescribes building designs based on celestial alignment and astrological principles. This knowledge directed the orientation and layout of buildings, aiming to optimize the flow of cosmic energy to promote prosperity and wellbeing.

Regardless of geographical location or the field in question, astrology continues to generate insights applicable to various practical domains of human life. As humans continue to find their place in the vast cosmic tapestry, the role of astrology, synchronizing the microcosm of humanity with the macrocosm of the universe, will always be irreplaceable. The secrets of the stars, as shared through astrology, have much to teach us about the world we inhabit and our place within it. We have indeed only just begun to scratch the surface of its expansively enlightening potential.

Chapter 9. Astrology Versus Astronomy: A Comparative Study

A hushed stillness falls over a room teeming with anticipation. The match begins as two contenders take their positions—Astrology, the ancient art interpreting cosmic patterns, and Astronomy, the scientific study of celestial objects. Like two sides of a celestial coin, each discipline grants us a unique perspective on our universe and our place within it. However, their methods and motivations vary as widely as the constellations in our night sky.

Chapter 10. Understanding Astrology: A Whisper of Fate

Let's begin with astrology, akin to the old sage whispering ancient fables beneath the starry sky—spinning tales not just of distant constellations, but of the impact they have on our lives. Human beings have been practicing astrology for thousands of years. Empires have risen and fallen guided by the secrets they believe the stars hold. Ancient Greeks and Romans ascribed patterns in the heavens to the gods' whims, while Chinese astrology involved complex cosmological theories and animal totems.

Astrology hinges on the presumption that celestial bodies, particularly the sun, moon, and planets, influence our personalities, behaviors, and circumstances. It's a perspective that builds on the intimate relationship between us and the cosmos, a dance that began when the first human looked skyward with wonder, pondering their connection to the celestial bodies.

Astrology's basic building blocks include the sun signs (determined by your birth date), moon signs, and rising signs. Using these elements, enhanced by the positions of the planets at the time of birth, an astrologer could construct an incredibly detailed birth chart. They interpret it almost like a cosmic blueprint, influencing everything from personality traits to future events.

Chapter 11. The Science of Astronomy: Probing the Depths of the Cosmos

In contrast, astronomy stands as a younger, restless scholar armed with a telescope. It is a science, after all, built on concrete evidence and rigorous experimentation. While astrology seeks to interpret, astronomy simply aims to observe, quantify, and understand.

Astronomy is the scientific study of celestial bodies like stars, planets, comets, and galaxies, as well as the phenomena that occur outside Earth's atmosphere. The discipline is driven by curiosity about the universe's fundamental laws and a ceaseless endeavor to learn more about our cosmic neighborhood.

Astronomers, like astrologers, observe patterns in the skies. However, these patterns serve as clues to the physical properties of celestial bodies and their histories, not human destinies. For example, redshifts and blueshifts in the light of distant galaxies led astronomers to deduce the universe's expansion—providing empirical support for the Big Bang theory.

Chapter 12. Astrology and Astronomy: Emergence and Divergence

The paths of astrology and astronomy, while divergent now, were not always so. Once upon a time, these disciplines were virtually indistinguishable. The observations that led to our modern understanding of celestial mechanics and the heavenly bodies fostered astrology's first steps.

However, as the scientific method began to reshape our understanding of the universe in the 17th century, astronomy emerged as a distinct field. It rapidly became a beacon of empirical truth, casting astrology's predictive suppositions into its lengthening shadow. Yet, despite the seemingly clear dichotomy, the relationship between astrology and astronomy isn't entirely one of disdain. Many astronomers appreciate the historical repository of knowledge of the night sky that astrology provides.

Chapter 13. A Comparison: Tools, Techniques, and Tenets

Perhaps one visible difference between astrology and astronomy lies in the tools they employ. An astrologer's toolkit includes star maps, ephemeris (charts detailing planetary motions), birth charts, and, most importantly, historical texts and interpretative abilities. In sharp contrast, astronomers tend to favor telescopes, observatories, mathematical models, and modern computational tools.

While both disciplines observe the heavens, their goals bear stark contrasts. For astrology, observation helps discern how celestial movements correlate with human life. Conversely, for astronomers, these observations elucidate understanding the components, processes, and evolution of the universe.

Despite the stark differences, both astrology and astronomy engage those who indulge in them with a sense of wonder, stimulating inquiry about the cosmos' mysteries. They draw us away from our presuppositions and everyday trivialities, compelling us to consider our place in the swathes of infinity that is our universe.

Chapter 14. Conclusion: A Stellar Parley

In a tumultuous debate between astrology and astronomy, there can be no definitive victor, as each discipline fulfills a unique role. We must remember, dispute aside, that both astrology and astronomy encourage us to raise our eyes to the stars with profound curiosity and mesmerizing wonder.

Astrology provides a touch of mysticism, an individual interpretation of the universe translated into personal guidance. Astronomy, on the other hand, is an empirical adventure, probing to answer the most intriguing questions about the cosmos, our home within it, and our celestial neighbors.

In the grand puzzle that is the universe, astrology and astronomy are two contrasting pieces. They may not fit together as they once did, but they both celebrate and interrogate our enduring fascination with the cosmos. Nothing connects us to the universe more than studying its infinite depths, whether through the lens of scientific inquiry or the eyes of personal interpretation.

Chapter 15. The Predictive Power of Astrology: Can It Tell Your Future?

Astrology, a celestial compass steering the journey of life, has long intrigued humans. Its interpretive power and predictive capacities challenge us to redefine our understanding of time, space, and fate. Throughout the ages, astrology's predictive power has been subjected to intense scrutiny, hailed by believers and scoffed at by skeptics. Yet, despite the discordant voices, its existential allure endures, fascinating us and drawing us into its cosmic orbit. This chapter will closely dissect the predictive power of astrology, delving deep into the methodologies astrologers employ to decipher the lucid whispers of the celestial bodies and how these cosmic insights can illuminate the road ahead.

15.1. The Mechanisms Behind Astrological Predictions

Astrology's predictive capabilities rely on two fundamental principles: the symbolic significance ascribed to celestial bodies, and their geometric relationship, or aspects.

Celestial bodies, including the sun, moon, planets, and certain points in space, are thought to represent different facets of our core being. The sun sign illustrates our central personalities, while the moon sign reflects our emotional skin. The ascendant, the zodiac sign on eastern horizon at our birth time, shows our outward persona.

In interpreting the celestial map, astrologers pay significant attention to the angular relationships between these celestial entities, known as aspects. Depending on the degree of separation, aspects can range from conjunctions (0 degrees), to oppositions (180 degrees), each carrying a distinct symbolic meaning influencing life events or experiences. The nature of the aspect- harmonious or tense- also influences predictions.

Among these aspects: *Conjunctions (0 degrees): Celestial bodies side by side, amplifies their energy. *Oppositions (180 degrees): Two entities at opposite poles, representing challenges leading to awareness. *Squares (90 degrees): Represents tension but ignite motivation. *Sextiles (60 degrees): Conducive for growth and opportunity. *Trines (120 degrees): Denote natural talent and ease.

Astrologers also work with transits, the current positions of planets compared to where they were at the individual's birth time, often used in forecasting.

15.2. Astrological Houses and Predictive Power

Envision your birth chart as a wheel, divided into twelve sections: these are the houses. Every house signifies a different life area, from money, to relationships, to career, to self-identity. During transits, planets move around the houses, their energy interacting with the life area they traverse. The nature of predictions depends on the entering planet, the house, and the planet it interacts with.

For instance, if Jupiter – the benefic planet representing growth and expansion – were to transit your second house of wealth, astrologers might predict a prosperous phase.

15.3. Astrology and Timing

Timing is a critical component of astrology's predictive power. Astrologers utilize different techniques to foresee when particular events may occur, two of which are:

*Primary Directions: Envisioning the celestial sphere as a giant clock, astrologers assess where planets are "directed" over time.

*Secondary Progressions: Here, each day following birth represents one year of life, providing insights into individual growth.

15.4. Astrology and Personal Transformation

Astrology is a robust instrument for personal growth. Transiting Pluto, for instance, can foretell eras of intense transformation, nudging you to shed old skin. Saturn's return, often felt around ages 29 and 59, often ushers periods of maturity and hard-earned lessons.

15.5. Skepticism Surrounding Astrology's Predictive Power

Many contend that the predictive power of astrology lacks empirical backing. Critics argue predictions are worded broadly, fitting numerous scenarios, an effect termed "The Forer Effect."

15.6. The Prerequisite Intention in Astrology

It is essential to approach astrology with the right intent. Astrology serves as a tool for introspection and self-understanding, rather than a rigid, deterministic blueprint of life. Understanding celestial influences can improve decision making and self-awareness, forging a more aligned path through life's journey.

In conclusion, astrology's predictive power manifests differently for every individual, depending on their unique natal chart. It doesn't necessarily prescribe events but highlights potential patterns and themes based on celestial interactions. While the future remains a mystery, astrology provides an intriguing lens through which to navigate the ebbs and flows of our journey, with the cosmos as our guide.

Chapter 16. Astrology Today: Its Impact and Influence in Modern Society

Astrology has firmly planted its roots in the soil of modern society, altering the landscape of our thoughts, our perspectives, and even our daily routines. It has transitioned from being an arcane practice, often dismissed as mere superstition, to a culturally accepted exploration of individual identities and the world around us. So impactful is its presence that the very mention of astrology often ignites passionate delight among adherents and equally fervent skepticism among skeptics.

16.1. Relevance in Contemporary Era

The resurgence of astrology in the modern society may seem sudden, like a star shooting across the night sky, but its influence has been quietly building for decades. The advent of the internet has nurtured astrology, allowing it to thrive through easy access to birth charts and daily horoscopes, expansive forums for individuals to discuss astrological phenomena and trends, and even dedicated apps offering personalized celestial insights. Whole communities have been birthed and blossomed in virtual spaces, connecting people from different corners of the globe with a shared interest in how the cosmic dance influences human existence.

Astrology in the 21st century has morphed into an interweaving of cultural currents: a tool for self-awareness, a framework for interpersonal understanding, and a guide for navigating life's unpredictable waters. The appeal lies not just in the search for answers but in the invitation to explore the broad spectrum of human experience. It encourages introspection, empathy, and a deeper awareness about the interconnectedness of all things.

16.2. Astrology and Self-Discovery

Astrology's role in self-discovery forms a crucial pillar of its staying power in the contemporary era. Many individuals approach astrology as a roadmap for personal understanding. Birth charts, in particular, serve as cosmic fingerprints, detailing the unique celestial configuration at the time of a person's birth. More than just determining sun signs, they reveal the placement of all the planets within the twelve houses, imparting potential insights about traits, passions, challenges, and personal growth opportunities.

Astrology offers a language with which individuals can articulate their experiences and explore their identities. It enables us to carve out our narrative, wielding the dance of the stars as a tool for self-discovery and self-fulfillment.

16.3. Astrology and Relationships

Astrology's application extends to our relationships with others, offering a framework for understanding interpersonal dynamics. Astrological compatability, explored through synastry, provides a celestial lens through which we can see patterns of attraction, challenge, and growth within our interactions. It encourages empathy by highlighting the different motivations, needs, and perspectives that each sign brings to the table.

While astrology does not prescribe determinism, it does offer illuminating insights that can foster better communication, mutual understanding, and more enriching relationships. It invites us to consider that the variabilities and complexities of human interactions may also bear the imprint of the cosmos.

16.4. Astrology as a Guide

Astrology is often turned to as a guide during times of uncertainty. The planetary movements, their aspects and transits, and how they interact with individual natal charts are seen as indicative of potential challenges and opportunities lying ahead. Numerous individuals observe and consider these celestial events when making major life decisions, from career moves to starting a new relationship.

While critics argue this can lead to a fatalistic mindset, proponents of astrology contend that it encourages proactive engagement with life's ups and downs. They see astrology not as a fixed forecast, but as guidance that can empower individuals to more consciously navigate the course of their lives.

16.5. Astrology and Mental Health

Interestingly, astrology has found a place within discussions of mental health. For some, it offers a non-threatening platform to explore and talk about personal struggles, emotional wellbeing, and self-improvement. This does not replace professional psychological help, but can be a significant complementary tool facilitating greater self-understanding and aiding articulation of thoughts and feelings.

16.6. Conclusion

The impact of astrology in modern society is multidimensional, extending into various aspects of our lives. Its influence persists because it continually evolves, adapting to address humanity's eternal questions about self, relationships, and purpose. From self-identity to relationships, from decision-making to mental health, astrology provides a multicolored lens through which modern society perceives and understands the world.

While the debate about astrology's validity is set to continue, its cultural significance is undeniable. The very fact that millions of individuals across the globe turn to astrology as a tool for understanding and guiding their lives testifies to its deeply rooted place in modern society. As we journey through the 21st century, swept by tides of technological advancement and social change, the celestial map offered by astrology remains a valuable tool for many navigating these waves.

Astrology, in its modern incarnation, embraces complexity and human diversity, and remains an intriguing lens through which society gazes at the universe, searches for light amid the cosmic darkness, and seeks to unravel the intricate dance between the stars and our human lives. It is a shared cosmic language, enabling us to explore the universe within us, as well as the universe beyond us.